THE
REPLACEABLE
FUNDER

ARI **MEISEL**

ACKNOWLEDGMENT

I'd like to acknowledge Amy Randall, without whom, this pinnacle work would never have materialized.

Courtney Waid, without whom, this impactful, inspiring content would never have existed.

Joanna Strange, without whom, Less Doing would not have reawakened to become the unstoppable force it is today.

Every day, they teach me the "how" of being The Replaceable Founder.

My wife Anna, who reminds me of the of "what" it means to live the life of The Replaceable Founder

My children, Benjamin, Lucas, Sebastien, and Chloe, who show me "why" I will always be The Replaceable Founder

FOREWORD

Before I met Ari Meisel, I had known about him simply because I found the idea of the service he and his business offer enormously attractive. With a simple phone call or online interaction, you can get in touch with Ari and his team and identify someone you need, someone who has skills that you don't have personally, skills that your team doesn't have.

Through digital networks, Ari and his team will find freelancers who can do this work. Not only that, they'll manage the project for you, help you clarify the project, and actually see the project through to its completion.

And it struck me immediately that this was something that we'd certainly recommend to our Strategic Coach clients.

Ari's brilliant at coaching people how to optimize, automate, and outsource, and to see things differently.

We've recommended that dozens of projects be communicated to Ari, and he's been knocking every single one of them out of the ballpark.

What fascinates and motivates you.

At Strategic Coach, we believe that you should only be doing what you love doing, what fascinates and motivates you, and what gives you energy.

Any activities that don't meet these criteria are either only okay for you, or actively negative and draining.

What happens to a lot of founders of entrepreneurial companies is that once they've built up organizations around them, they start taking on activities that are necessary but that aren't in their area of unique capability and passion.

Not only is this not good for the individual, it also means that the founder is spending less time doing what it is they're best at: coming up with ideas to make themselves, their company, and their clients bigger and better than they are right now.

Paying customers are excited about the new things you introduce to the marketplace, and they want to see your ideas keep getting better. It's important to avoid getting tied into the organization you've created instead of this powerful, dynamic marketplace value creation relationship.

Create the electricity instead of getting focused on the wiring.

Freeing you up.

The goal and game plan of any ambitious entrepreneur is to always be replacing themselves with a team and company that manages itself to greater growth, freeing you up to focus on the bigger vision.

For each person you're thinking about hiring, make sure to ask yourself, "Is this person another building block toward my company becoming increasingly self-managing?" In other words: "What part of my existing process can this person manage in such a way that my time doesn't have to be spent doing it?"

As a result, if you hire someone and it increases the amount of management you do, that's not a good hire.

"Who" not "How."

Whenever a business owner does the "how" of a project themselves instead of finding a more capable "who," they'll find it frustrating and tiring, and they'll also become a bottleneck to progress and growth.

As the entrepreneur, all of your time should be freed up from implementation so you can be constantly creating greater and greater value out in the marketplace. Other people can use their own unique capabilities to handle the mechanics that support what you do.

The role of the entrepreneurial founder is to envision a bigger and better result than they have now, and then coming back and communicating that vision effectively to the people who can actually take the actions that will produce the result.

The founder's job is to define the "what" and the "why" of the project— *"This is what it is, and this is why it's so important"*—in such a way that it's persuasive and motivating, and to find the team of specialists and experts who are gifted at completing the various parts of the project. And then to do this over and over again.

You don't have to control the "how" of the work getting done. After communicating the bigger and better idea to the right people for the job, the founder should always be then moving onto the next bigger and better idea.

It's vitally important that your ideas are shared and multiplied. All long-term entrepreneurial success depends on individuals replacing existing solutions with new breakthrough innovations, and this is the entrepreneurial founder's territory.

A thought leader.

What I've noticed when Ari coaches at conferences, and when he's in his Strategic Coach workshops, is that he really makes it clear that an entrepreneurial founder who endlessly performs the same activities and doesn't delegate has put themselves on a treadmill, where there's lots of activity but no progress.

Ari has established himself within the entrepreneurial world as the key thought leader in creating an endlessly expanding network of skilled "who's" to do the "how's."

Out of all the people I've worked with over my 45 years of coaching successful entrepreneurs, Ari has the greatest clarity and the greatest capability to help entrepreneurial business owners and founders to design a plan that combines both greater teamwork and greater technology to actually make themselves replaceable—not in the sense that they're not needed, but in the sense that they're now freed up to go to a higher level.

With this book, Ari has created a blueprint of how companies get big in the 21st century, and he's created a guide for you to be able to grow more quickly, with less pain involved.

Dan Sullivan, Founder of The Strategic Coach®, Inc.

TABLE OF CONTENTS

INTRODUCTION

T he market is saturated with really innovative books and philosophies about growth; how to find new opportunities, how to create new content and marketing, how to identify and nurture customers. Entrepreneurs especially have endless choices these days when they are pursuing those solutions.

"The Replaceable Founder" is not that book.

This book will assist you in uncovering what is holding you back, and find where your constraints hide. It will show you the relevance of becoming replaceable.

It's a daunting word, for sure, but it does not mean what you think it does. My methodology does not seek to make you disappear; it aims to give you the time and space to truly lead.

It is, after all the bottlenecks we are trying to avoid as we nurture our vision. The truth is excellent ideas shepherded by brilliant people will usually succeed. In Latin, *ceteris paribus* which translates to "all other things being equal."

So this book is about the constraints that impede progress, and it's been my experience that the obstacle is usually the founder. It is this person, the one who came up with the brilliant idea, the one who wants to get it done, yesterday, that becomes their own worst enemy. They may rush to bring their aha moment to bear, and then bring in the wrong people to help. They buy cumbersome and ill-fitting software, and they don't put the proper systems in place first; processes that reflect and support the mission of the organization. These hasty decisions mar progress and erode the company's DNA and those breaks in the DNA multiply untethered throughout the evolution of that organization.

What remains, several months or years into a venture, is an overwhelmed founder with too much to do, not enough time to accomplish anything significant, and an attitude of defeat which will surely spell the demise of a terrific idea. If the founder is spending their time like this, they are detracting rather than adding value to the initial offering. They will fail, and more importantly, they will not know why.

The solution lies in a fundamental shift in mindset whose hallmark is, "Everyone should be as replaceable as possible." I do not mean personally, I mean professionally. It doesn't mean firing; it means optimizing processes so that people, especially the founder are free to drive their vision forward and this is impossible to do if they are mired in the daily grind of putting out fires.

The objective must be to replace the HOW. Not the WHAT and the WHY.

Naturally, the founder should be spearheading the mission of why but the how needs to focus on replacement, making everyone as replaceable as possible, without actually replacing them.

Remember, the founder's team has a wealth of knowledge and experience. They wouldn't have been hired to help grow a business if they didn't possess these talents. Their unique gifts continue to be more and more valuable every day they are with an organization. The core team is invested in the vision, has a passionate and proprietary interest in its success, but like the founder they are spending too much of their time doing things that could be done by someone else, faster and for less.

If the founder is paying his Marketing guru to post on Instagram, they are wasting money. If the accounts person is personally answering customer queries, they are drowning in inefficiency and if the founder is unable to relinquish control to anyone outside the core team, productivity halts.

I realize that to many people, this may sound like a paradox, a double edge sword. "If I make myself replaceable, I'll just replace myself out of a job!" Admittedly, in many organizations I've worked with, there are those who can't or won't see that finding an optimized solution enables, rather than disables. But the people who do embrace the notion can fill that empty space with new and better opportunities.

It's the opposite of *The Peter Principle*, the satirical book about incompetence, written by Laurence J. Peter and Raymond Hull in 1969, that heralded the notion that people rise to the point of their incompetence. Peter and Hull uncovered the lunacy of traditional corporate structures that only promoted based on a person's ability to do the job they currently held, which left many within the organizational structure over their heads in positions they were incapable of mastering, rendering them obsolete.

My view and I've seen it work countless times, is to get to a position, through optimizing, automating, and outsourcing, where the founder, in particular, is now able to step up into that void and get shit done. Real shit. Substantive shit. Shit that turns that great idea into a brilliant triumph.

The mantra must be:

Become replaceable.

Seek out the constraints.

Remove the bottleneck.

Allow the natural growth to happen.

Let's begin.

CHAPTER ONE

THE PRICE OF DISRUPTION

My friend, Joe Polish, drops truth bombs a lot. One that resonates with me is the adage that as founders we need to see ourselves as the first domino; not the only domino, just the beginning. We must be the person who initiates the chain reaction that leads to growth.

However, to do that, we need to stop looking for the "how" and instead look for the "who." It's a subtle but profound distinction. As founders, we don't need to know how to do something; how to build a CRM, how to automate processes, how to create a social media presence. We need to know who can do that work, and by who I mean...not you.

In practice, it can be as simple as off-loading some repetitive task that eats up your day to a virtual assistant or finding a person who can write, design or produce content better than you.

Yet, those solutions act only as band-aids if you haven't taken the time to assess your business and look into the dark corners of counterproductive systems and processes.

When it comes to this type of deep-dive into the machinations of your business, a great deal of fortitude is required. Unless we are open to the notion that someone else, with a drone-like perspective, is the only person objective enough to solve our most significant challenges, we'll stall or sink. We must get out of our own way. We must find the next domino and then let it go.

When I'm asked to embark on this kind of discovery with a client, I require two things...willingness and an open mind. Resistance is futile, and a vice-grip hold on, "the way we do things around here," can lead to disaster.

So, the process is not for the faint of heart, because my team and I ask, "Why"? A lot.

We challenge conventional wisdom and upend entrenched ideas about what works, what doesn't, what's antiquated and what's innovative. Sure there's contention, fear and push back. We wouldn't be human if we didn't, to varying degrees, resist change. However, in the end, if a team can see the OAO benefits we provide, the dominos begin to fall.

So, instead of telling you how we do it, I've asked a few clients to speak for themselves about the parts of the journey that resonated with them the most. Their thoughts introduce the chapters that pertain to an aspect of the OAO Methodology. These two case studies are from two very different businesses, but they shared a common dilemma....The inability to make progress.

As you read through their stories, resist the urge to compare your business to theirs. Instead, look to identify the commonalities, the threads that resonate with you. Once you see your own business struggles, in the stories they tell, you can begin to embrace the solutions.

And that is the price of disruption.

CHAPTER TWO

MALTE HOLM - LETTING IT GO

"I think the personal part of productivity or lack of it, is the springboard into fixing your business and leaving that part out doesn't do us any good...at least that's been my experience."

I became CEO four years ago. I used to be on a board of directors for a big holding company. It was a very different kind of life. When I transitioned into my current role, there was a lot more on my plate; a new team, the need to change a lot of things and me, quite honestly, felt like I was going a bit crazy.

I have two small kids, and I didn't want to be that CEO that was doing well economically, super successful, but never there for my family.

So I wanted to do things the right way. However, I didn't know what it was. Obviously, you can hire a team, but we could not do that in the beginning. We were strapped for cash.

So it came back to, "How do I balance family and work life in a way where I still get everything done?

I started using a VA company, and I thought well, this is cool. However, it's was so difficult to get started. What do I outsource? Will they be able to do it better than me? So I started watching Ari's coaching calls and pretty quickly I found myself with this new mindset.

I had to learn what I was doing first, to tell someone else how to do it. It seems simple now, but it was incredibly difficult in the beginning.

However, little by little you train your mind to look at the process objectively first, not just give it away because you can't be bothered.

I think for me that was the problematic part, in the beginning, just trying to figure out what to give away. So, I realized I needed coaching and experimentation. My resistance was that a process like that has a cost. You can either hire someone, use a VA for a task but it would cost me. However, I came to learn that it's an insufficient way of looking at optimization.

Because if we only look at it as how much it's going to cost, we don't see it as an opportunity. There are so many ways you can take a company, so many things you could do with your family, and you're just not doing all that because you can only do one thing at a time. So I took the KOLBE test to figure out who I was, and why I was resistant to any number of solutions. What I discovered is that I'm not the one who hesitates, who isn't up for trying new things, but my ego was standing in the way. I wanted to be the one to handle everything, and it was quickly becoming a disaster.

So I hired a dedicated VA pretty fast.

In El Salvador, you can hire a VA for about $7.50/hour. They don't have the skills of VA services who charge more, but I had to start. It was pretty messy in the beginning. So I think figuring out what to delegate, taking the time to look at my processes. I had to ask myself, Is there any way that person can make a particular task easier? I think the struggle for a lot of us is that we come from a mindset where we think we don't have the time to take the time to explain a task. Right? It's like that chicken or the egg where you're so busy that I can't figure out how to not be busy, which is crazy.

So I started making the time. It was very tough because it seemed like every time I did that, the company was falling in sales and some project we wanted to launch we couldn't. However, I had to take time off to get my act together and figure out not only what could be outsourced but what could be done differently and what my team might need.

I figured out that I needed a more robust team, overseeing the whole operation left me no time to think about the big things. I couldn't run the day to day and develop the strategy. It was impossible.

So I invested the time to get more time. I memorialized our processes for everything. Even though a lot of it felt instinctual, there was repetition and quantitative data. I stopped saying, well I don't know why I do it that way, I do and it works out. Once I memorialized it, I could let it go, and that felt amazing.

The tendency for founders and entrepreneurs is to be more right-brainers. We all come up with good ideas. However, processes bore me. Processes are not natural. So I think for guys like me, we need to recognize that we need a helping hand. The theory is one thing. Practice is another. Having someone guide you through it makes it so much easier the first time.

I think obviously it comes back to mindfulness. I have done a lot of psychographic testing, and I love those kinds of things because it's fun to learn about oneself and other people. What it confirmed for me is that I'm good at innovation, but I suck at executing. I can't tell you how helpful that information has been for me and my business.

The tools are very liberating as long as you're not afraid of the liberation. For example, I had a CFO that left the company early on. We did not replace him, because I did not need him. I simply needed bookkeeping that could give me the analytics I knew how to read. We found that by really looking at the process, we just needed a fundamental analysis of the numbers.

So accounting gives us the numbers, and we need to study the impacts. I didn't need a full-time person overseeing that.

The key to all of this I think is that you are taking people with enormous egos and telling them that they have to relinquish their ego to become more successful. You are going to have people who have entirely resistant to that. However, the moment you abandon that control is the moment you have more control over your life, which is a complete paradox and challenging to understand.

But it works.

Here's a great example. I asked my head of HR how much time she spent in traffic every day because it seemed like the process of getting to work was hard. "She said no one had ever asked her that question, but she figured about four hours a day". I was amazed, and kind of distressed She said, well, you told me you needed me here at 8 AM every day. Well, what time would you like to leave your house to get here faster? What if you worked from home? Well, she didn't have internet at home, so we set her up with a simple broadband, and now she can do just about everything she needs to do from home. It has made her a much more productive and committed employee. However, I never would have known the solution, if I didn't ask the question. I had to relinquish this idea that employees needed to be in their seats working in front of me every day.

Now I feel like I'm enabling people to honestly express themselves because their life is their own. I trust that the work will get done and the process of letting go has allowed me to become much more productive as well.

We as founders have to take the time to be mindful and ask, "What's really important for you?" The majority of the world's population will never ask themselves that question. That's just living on auto-pilot, and it's so counter-productive. But then you have to ask yourself, How can I use my company as a platform for that and find meaning, real meaning, not just money, for you and those around you.

The notion that because we live in this entrepreneurial world of fast everything, we can't ever pause and be present, is bullshit. Because understanding what you can and cannot deal with at any given moment is the only way to move it forward. It takes you entirely out of reactive mode and puts you in a much more realistic mindset. Putting out fires may stoke your ego, but it's a doesn't move anything forward. In fact, it's a complete waste of time. Nothing in an optimized business should ever be on fire, and in the rare instances where there is a fire, you have a process to deal with it. It should be a rarity. Never a daily occurrence.

Still, the methodology requires a massive level of commitment in all honesty. It's like building muscle. It's not something you can decide on having and automatically have it. It takes work, and it's not comfortable or pretty in the beginning. There is no quick fix. But if you stick with the process, you only have to be a beginner once.

CHAPTER THREE

INBOX ZERO

I speak all over the world, and when I ask audiences what their single greatest productivity challenge is, the vast majority say....wait for it.... their email. Hands down. So let's talk about email, because email is not the problem.

I have a friend who surfs, and she says people always ask her, "How many waves did you catch today?" and she always answers, "that's not the point." It's the same thing with email. Email is not the point; it's your ability or inability to make decisions.

Now don't worry I'm going to teach you in this chapter to take control of your email and get and stay at inbox zero, but first I need to give you some context. The lesson in getting to inbox zero is all about learning to make better decisions, something a founder needs every day. You need to stop getting bogged down in the details that prevent you from scaling, and it all starts with email. Really.

Your inbox gives you a unique opportunity to make thousands of decisions in a day. However, the problem with the typical inbox, which is not unlike the usual sort of business operation, is that there are many different kinds of decisions happening simultaneously and relentlessly. Essential and optional intermingle.

Just take a moment now and look at how many emails you have in your inbox right now? Write it down somewhere, because when you are finished with this chapter, I want you to go back and see how much the number will change. Spoiler alert...it will. A lot. So let's begin successfully managing your inbox by controlling information that comes into it and systematically tackling the requests we receive.

I'm tool agnostic, so I don't care what we use to get it done, but I care about how you think. This exercise is all about mindset. It's not useful to learn what successful people do or how they do it. It's one of the reasons I'm not too fond of things like, "The Seven Habits of Highly Successful People or the Seven Things" that most Successful People Never Do in the Morning. Those habits are what they do. It's not how they think. It's better to learn what successful people do. To do that you need to learn how they think. Let's use that perspective now.

The first thing is email is your tool, like your phone and your laptop. Many people think about these tools as ways for the outside world to get a hold of them and at the end of the day, that's what they end up being. They end up being leashes for the outside world. 24/7. However, these are your tools and you get to decide how to use them.

By the way, you don't have to use email. While there are many businesses where that would make things extremely difficult, there are some very, very successful people in the world who have never used email. John Paul DeJoria is one example. He is the creator of Paul Mitchell hair products. He's worth about $3,000,000,000. He's never had an email; he's never used a computer.

So it is your choice, and it's your tool, and you have to use it the way that suits you.

Secondly, email is an asynchronous communication tool, meaning that you can use it to write and respond when it is right for you. So can anyone else. There is no right or wrong time to check your email and people who say they only check it twice a day, are lying. I check my email probably 40 times a day. I love checking my email because I have an efficient email inbox and it's a place of action, activity, interest and a place where I can get shit done. So use it the way you want, when you want.

Remember it doesn't matter what you're doing in the inbox: answering a question, providing a biography, or viewing a document, activity becomes email; even if you're dealing with 15 types of different micro activities. If you understand that the actual overall work that you're doing is email inboxes, then that becomes your focal point. The number of times that you sign in is not as important as how much time you spend processing. If you have an efficient decision process in place, then it doesn't matter how often you're checking it because you could check it for a few seconds and get something done as long as you're not taking that thought with you to the next activity.

So why is inbox zero important?

Well, the inbox is your tool, and right now many people are using the inbox as an open-ended "to do" lists that other people fill for you. So email is not the problem. It's how you manage it.

How you do anything is how you do everything.

If you are not able to effectively manage your inbox, it reflects poorly on you as a manager. If somebody responds to me after two or three or four weeks and says, "Well, I'm sorry, I missed your email." That to me says, I'm dealing with an incredibly inefficient person, and I think that's more telling than almost anything else. Looking at somebody's inbox is like a window into their soul. You can tell a lot about somebody by the way they manage or mismanage their inbox.

So if you have an email in your inbox that is not answered within two weeks, I would argue that it at that point you should not respond. You should pretend that it's been lost because it's almost ruder to respond. Two weeks is a lifetime, nowadays. So archive it. Now that doesn't mean to delete it, that means it's out of your inbox.

Next, we want to create a rule in Gmail, for example, to filter our incoming mail. Create a filter that looks for the word "unsubscribe," and it will find the word and send it to elsewhere, completing avoiding your inbox. Again, If it has the word "unsubscribe" it goes directly to your archive.

So I know that a lot of you are thinking, "Oh, no. What if there's this newsletter that I liked to read every day?" My answer is, "That's fine, but realistically are you finding the time each day to read that newsletter to take advantage of that content? Because if you're not, it should not be cluttering up your inbox. You can always go into the archive folder at the end of the day when you have some time and very quickly scan through it. Remember we are training our brains to think differently about how we use our time.

Psychologically, the inbox is a place of action; there are things in there that are essential; that you need to do, but you need to get in the mindset that everything else that's in there is optional. You don't need to deal with it. You don't need to get to it. It's not part of your daily thing.

My mantra when it comes to email is threefold. Only three decisions are available.

DO

DELETE

DEFER

So you know about the phrase, "Always Be Closing", I prefer, "Always Be Done." How can we do something right now, in the moment, at this point so that we can be done? We overthink about what to do and waste too much time procrastinating and stressing. We can make it so that every decision that we make, every action that we take, will have some progress attached to it. I always want to move forward, because even when we're moving forward, and we make some wrong decisions, we will still be in a new place where we can make a new decision. Hopefully, it will be the right one.

If you do it now, do it right now, not only will you feel the dopamine rush, but actual micro goals will be completed. You will no longer be the bottleneck. Imagine the game hot potato. You get the potato. You have just enough time to understand that it's HOT and you quickly pass it off to someone or something else. As a leader you need to be doing that, touch it as little as necessary.

So the "DO" decision answers the question, "What are the things you should take care of right now? Tasks that will take no more than five minutes and functions that need to be delegated.

The challenge for many is the delegating piece. However, giving direction should take five minutes or less. Say it once, to the right person (or platform) at the right time. However, to make this work, you have to have some system in place before you delegate. Again, being a leader, your job is to direct the flow of energy, not impede it.

The second option is to DELETE it. You should be saying no to more than you are. I don't care what situation you're in, your life and your business, you must be able to say no to things that don't serve your higher goal.

You do not need to write back to that email and say, "Thanks. Got It". The more email you write, the more email you will get. It's the boomerang effect. It's like the high school boyfriend and girlfriend on the phone saying, "You hang up." "No, you hang up." "No, you hang up." The more you say, the more someone will respond. No could also mean that you hand it off to somebody else that's a colleague, another company, another competitor even it doesn't matter, because, for you, it's a No.

So if you can't do it right now, then you have the third option, DEFER it. We all have our peak times (see APPENDIX for more info). We each have good times and bad times to engage in specific activities. It's OK to say, I can't do that now, but Tuesday at 10:00 AM is excellent, or I'll be able to work on this tonight. Whatever it might be, it's crucial to know that deferring and procrastinating is not the same. Procrastination is a fear-based activity where you're just pushing away something you don't want to commit to doing. Whereas deferring requires that you take an active role. You are taking ownership and saying now is not the time but "X" time is when you can get it done and get it done well.

So if I need to do creative work, I'm not going to jam that in between doing financial stuff or a brainstorming session with my team. No one can switch mental focus like that and claim that they are efficient. If I need to write something, (like this book), I know I have a peak time for that kind of work. 8 PM and it's the only activity I'm doing. Then I don't think about it again until 8 PM.

Tasks in your inbox can be deferred to another time AND place. Commonly, I do this when I travel. I'll defer things to an airport; my local airport if it's something I know that I want to do on the plane, or a destination airport if someone says to me for example, "You should check this out next time you're in Detroit, and I have no idea when I'm going to be in Detroit next. So I'll snooze that item to the Detroit airport. Google will send me a notification then. Cool right?

The InBox Zero Steps.

1. Create a filter that weeds out emails with the word "Unsubscribe."
2. Establish whether the emails that remain fall under:
   a. Do - Can this be dealt with or delegated in five minutes?
   b. Delete - Does this require a response?

      c. Defer - Is there a more productive time or place to tackle this?

CHAPTER FOUR

IDEA CAPTURE

L et's talk about organizing ideas.

In this chapter, you'll learn how to eliminate distraction and improve focus; how to set up an idea capture system, how to put it into practice and how to implement this methodology as a cultural cornerstone with your team and organization.

Honestly, it's a lot easier than it sounds.

Sure, we all want ideas to flow, and if we can dampen the internal noise and find a way to memorialize those ideas, it's possible to get to this incredibly productive place, where time is irrelevant. We are working on something we love without distraction. To me, adopting this process is a crucial step toward becoming replaceable.

The necessary mindset shift here is committing to the idea that there are different times to come up with ideas and other times to process them. A founder who thinks they are one in the same is a founder who cannot progress.

Granted, we have ideas all day long, and the human brain is fantastic at coming up with them, but we are not wired to hold on to them with any surety. So rather than battling with yourself, your memory, and your focus, separate those two functions.

It's easier said than done. But stay with me.

Entrepreneurs, in particular, tend to suffer from "shiny object syndrome." We get an idea and say, OMG, I'm going to stop and work on this amazing idea. It's interesting. It's exciting. I'm totally inspired right now. It's a recipe for disaster. So stop.

Instead, force yourself to stop thinking about it. Don't allow it to ruminate in your head. I know what you're thinking, but it's a genius idea, a game changer, how can I not think about it? I'll forget about it.

My answer is always the same; I didn't say you had to stop thinking about it, I'm just saying you can't do it now. Go ahead and capture everything from your aha moments to your grocery list, throughout the day like I do, but don't engage with them until you've carved out the time to process them. I do this at 8:00 PM because in my life, that's when things quiet down. I can breathe a little and think.

I'm no different from the average person in that my brain is a horrible judge.

It is set up in a way that is very defensive; a vestige of our primitive beginnings where our choices were, "kill or be killed". So, we tend to shoot down many ideas that could be good, because we are in a reactive mode most of the day.

The other aspect of our lizard brain is that we hold on too tight. You may have an idea right now that you think you must take advantage of, you must commit to memory. Fire good, wooly mammoths bad. However, we end up using our long-term working memory for this effectively blocking out any other work that needs to get done right in the moment. Pick berries, collect water.

So we end up with decision fatigue and are cognitively exhausted at the end of the day because we've tried to use our memories for the wrong thing at the wrong time.

If you've ever had a Blackberry, you may be familiar with the game, "Brick Breaker." I loved this game. There was a paddle across the bottom of the screen. You had to use the paddle to send a ball to hit the bricks. There were spaces on the side so you could run the ball so it went up the front of the bricks and broke a bunch of them at once.

The reason I mention this is because it's a bit like our ideas and what we do with them. You have to have control of it just long enough to determine what it is and where it needs to go. Then you can begin to sort. Is the idea going to a person? An automation? A process? Your goal is to avoid being a bottleneck and become more of a brick breaker.

OK, one more example. There's a great *Simpson's* cartoon episode where Homer doesn't want to learn some new things. Marge asks him to go to some class, and he says he doesn't want to learn. He says, "Every time I learn something new, I forget something else. Remember that time I took a winemaking class and then I forgot how to drive?" Marge says, "that's because you were drunk."

However, the truth is, Homer was right. We have a limited amount of space upstairs. We think we can do everything and want to try, but we can't. Our brains are not our friends in this pursuit. So we have to outsmart our minds a little bit. We are conditioned from a millennium of evolution to knock down anything that doesn't really help our survival or massively advance it. So that idea you just had, while reading this book, for some new Facebook ads, that you don't want to forget, You must stop chasing the idea down some rabbit hole that makes you lose focus. Just capture it and get back to reading this book.

I process an enormous amount of content every day. I follow about 20 or 25 different podcasts. There are 15 or 20 weekly newsletters a week I like to read. My conversations with both my team and my clients inspire me to come up with new ideas. Then, of course, there were situations where I'm presented with extreme limits to my resources. Usually, that involves one of my four children. I have a compressed workday, but I am never more than 20 seconds away from capturing an idea. I mean that literally.

The next thing is deciding where you want the idea to go. It gets subjective here because it depends on your individual preference and how you operate as an organization. Are you an audio-visual learner? Somebody who likes to read? Do you want ideas to come to you by text, by email? Do you want them to go right into a project management tool? Do you want them to go to another person who will discuss them with you at a weekly meeting? All of these are options, and no one is more valid than the other, but you have to decide first how best to process information. For me, it's an email digest at 8:00 at night. However, maybe you are a morning person who needs visual stimulation.

Pick a time and delivery method, and you're halfway there. For example, just because there is a symposium at 1:00 in a different time zone, doesn't mean that you must stop everything and attend. Set it up to receive that content at 9:00 at night sitting comfortably in your living room chair.

Now to connect the dots. Once we know where the ideas come from and we know where they're going, we have to figure out how they get there and what is the best pathway to use. It's called creating an "External Brain."

I define the external brain as something other than what's between your ears. Anywhere else you can drop ideas is better than letting then rumble around internally. It can be a voice message, a screenshot or merely forwarding an email. I strive to be a conduit for information, not a repository. You know why? ...because there's an app for that. It's called IFTTT, which stands for If This Then That. It's completely free to set up an account, and it works off a smooth trigger and action system. It ties in with hundreds of services that you use on a daily basis, and my only caveat is that scrolling through all the available "applets" or "recipes" can be a rabbit-hole in and of itself.

So once we get an account, pick a recipe with which to practice capturing ideas and saving them for a later time. Below are a few of my favorites and you can access them by searching for Less Doing on IFTTT's website.

liontex's Applets

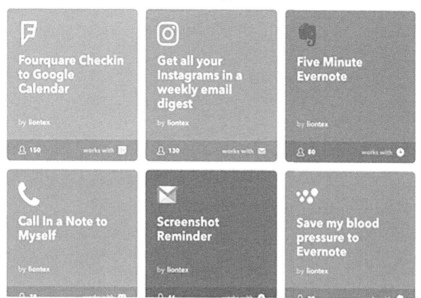

So let's create a screenshot on your phone, whether you're android or apple, it's basically at the same process. It takes about a 10th of a second to click that button and capture an idea. Be it a text message, a Facebook message, a podcast, email, a calendar, something I want to say; I can screenshot it in a 10th of a second and then forget about it because I know that it'll come to me later on as my digest. So the trigger is going to be new screenshot in my case. Then what do we want to happen? For me, it's a digest that I get at 8:00 at night. So the action sends the email digest daily. You can do it weekly if you want, but I do everyday.

CHAPTER FIVE

STRATEGIC COMMUNICATION

The world is waiting for you to interact with it, twenty-four hours a day. While that may seem grandiose or idealistic, the truth is no matter what the information is, where it's coming from, or who is sending it, you can control the way that you perceive it, process it and receive it.

My goal in this chapter is to help you separate the urgent from the non-urgent in your business and develop an effective system of communication for your team and your customers that fits seamlessly into your workflow.

Asynchronous communication may be the answer. It means you're going to have to start talking to yourself a lot more because this type of connection is not a two-way street. It is not live or directly with another human being. You may think that sounds robotic and insensitive, but structuring your communication system this way allows you to become more authentic, inspired and productive.

The tools we use must feel like they belong to us; that we can then use them however we like. Email, for example, is treated by many as a "To Do" list we fill out for other people. It's a mistake to allow a tool to tether us to the world. I think email is the greatest productivity tool ever invented, but I don't let people use it against me.

If you're working a nine to five job with particular requirements around that, it may not be within your control. Still, you can make adjustments to your approach that will make your work life a whole lot smoother.

Just because we have email doesn't mean that somebody can get to you whenever he or she wants. Moreover, just because somebody wants you to respond to them urgently, it's hardly ever necessary. Nothing that is truly urgent, should come through email. If somebody is emailing you something critical, then it's not urgent. In other words, if you got hit by a car, you wouldn't send an email letting your husband know.

I like to say as founders, we don't want to spend our days putting out fires. Granted, fires appear in the businesses we run, but that's not how we should be set up. We want to build a fireproof building and what that requires is a little bit of planning and a little bit of understanding about where information should go and how to sort it out most effectively.

The first piece of the puzzle is separating internal from external. So internal and external communications are indeed not the same, and it's usually why most inboxes are so overwhelming. External email tends to be very transactional, like communication with customers or clients, vendors or with outsiders.

"How long does it take you to ship these items?"

"It takes ten days."

or

"Can we set up a meeting?"

"Yes, and here are the times that we can do it."

Now internal communication tends to be more collaborative, more discussion-based. The reason that email stinks for this kind of conversation is that discussion is utterly ineffective when we have BCCs, forwards and CCs in twenty emails. It's a chain letter where you have no idea to whom you are even talking, and someone invariably goes off on a unrelated topic with its own set of asides.

I was sitting at a birthday party last weekend with my four-year-olds, and one of the dads noticed that I was using Voxer. (my preferred asynchronous form of communication. It's a next level walkie-talkie).

He asked me about it, and I told him. He said, "Oh, that's funny. Here's what I use at the UN. I use Viber for talk to the EU; I use Signal to talk domestically and Telegram for our missions in Asia. They are all incredibly secure but only for a particular region." It was so amazing to me. First of all that that these platforms were so secure and also that he had separate tools for separate kinds of communication.

You mentally switch when you're using a different tool for different kinds of communication. We need that compartmental approach because if you have everything in one place, you have to continually reset yourself, to accommodate to the different scenarios that come up. So some of the things you have to consider when you're separating out the various forms of communication are time zones and locations. In my former business, I had people in 17 times zones. It required an exceptional kind of planning and a clear company-wide understanding of what constituted "URGENT."

It is a big dilemma for many people. I subscribe to the Abraham Lincoln's idea of "Don't put off till tomorrow what you can do today," but that's not the same thing as being urgent. Urgent to me is when something is life-threatening; something that will end the business if it's not dealt with it right now.

Now, you might say that excellent customer service requires urgency. I disagree. Urgency to me implies poor planning. Think about that for a second. Urgency suggests poor planning. Now, of course, we cannot plan for everything, but not everything we believe to be urgent, actually is.

We need to do two things -- get better at planning and stop getting frenetic in "right now" situations. Yes, it may need to be dealt with right now, but that doesn't mean it is urgent. So if it's not urgent, doesn't even need to be discussed right now.

Also, remember that what may be urgent to one person is not necessarily crucial to the other. It's called "correspondence bias." It's a well-documented psychological state where you take somebody's behavior at the moment, and you apply it to their entire persona. Any behavior after that moment, reinforces your point-of-view. The best example of this is you're driving down the highway, and some person comes flying up and cuts you off. You think, "What that jerk." You''ll honk, try to cut them off, grumble or be angry because you're assuming that person did not just ACT like a jerk but IS a jerk.

However, what if they were on the way to the hospital because their wife was in labor?

In other words, the sense of urgency is perspective based. If you have something go wrong with a client, somebody who works for you might think, "Oh, it's urgent that I get this to the boss and figure this out."

Their urgency is driven by their assumptions about how you operate as a founder and their own place in the organization based on past experience. You can avoid this by setting guidelines and allowing people the space to solve their problems. When a person feels empowered, urgency dissipates.

So what's urgent and what's not? A former partner asked me what would constitute an emergency to me. The only thing I could think of was if somebody emptied our bank accounts. Urgent. General customer requests? Non-urgent. Brainstorming new initiatives? Important, but not urgent.

My business has been up and running for a little over a year now. We've grown fast and made all kinds of fundamental changes to our business model. We've never once had an urgent matter arise. Not once.

Now let's talk about your peak time. It's typically a 90 minute period of the day where you are two to 100 times more effective than any other time of the day. People are two to 100 times more likely to get into a flow state then. One of the experiences around a flow state is the dilation of time. So if you ever felt yourself in a situation where you felt hours passed and it like minutes, that was probably a form of a flow state for you.

So a quick way to figure this out is there is an app in the Google App store and on iTunes called the "Less Doing Peak Time" app. You tap your finger on the screen a few times a day as fast as you can. The experiment is based on something called "The Central Nervous System Tap Test." It allows you to identify the time of the day when your nervous system is firing on all cylinders. When you determine what and when that time is, block it off to the best of your ability and only use it for your highest and best work. The results will be staggering.

The critical thing is that you don't want that time to be interrupted by a non-urgent activity as I described earlier. For example, I know that our writer, Amy is NOT at her peak time between four and six pm. I'm not going to bug her with my idea. I'll use some asynchronous method like Voxer for example, that hopefully, she turns off during that time so that I can give her an idea and she doesn't have to act on it until later on.

So start to schedule your day and your team's day and the communications that you have around those various peak times. When do you want them to contact you and how do you want them to contact you? Set up the rules in advance. A little bit of planning goes a long way. We're talking about the things that happen in your business regularly. It's just planning and putting things in place.

Imagine a Venn diagram with two circles, slightly overlapping. One circle is synchronous and the other asynchronous. Now, the reason that there's a crossover here is that there are types of communication that could fall into both categories and part of that depends on the tool. Let's say a daily stand up can be asynchronous. VIP client issues, would be synchronous because we probably want to pick up the phone and talk about the issues. General requests. Those should be asynchronous. Somebody can ask a question in say, Intercom and somebody will get back to it at the right time. Now obviously the more responsive we can be, the better. But wouldn't it be terrible if somebody could walk into your office and say, "Hey, this just happened. Could you help me out right now?" Maybe you don't have any of the background information. Maybe it's unrelated to your core work. Maybe you're eating lunch. How could you possibly be expected to formulate a solution. With asynchronous communication, you can think about it, ruminate on it and develop a plan...in your own time.

There are tools I couldn't live without in my business. They're all communications channels. Like the 50 words for snow the Inuits have, it's an example of how important communication is to me.

Intercom allows us to turn email into a team sport. It effortlessly bridges the gap between internal and external communication. I can grab live chats from my website, receive text messages from clients or leads, get Facebook messages from my business page and all our company emails. They all come to one place, and then any team member can respond as needed. However, more importantly, it gives us that pause. We can discuss it internally (in Intercom) before reacting externally.

Slack is the internal communication tool that we love and where we brainstorm, make fun of each other and get guidance and support.

Voxer is a game changer for us. It's a free voice messaging app. So all of my ideas, all day long, get sent out and no one is being interrupted. I'm not walking down the hallway popping into Courtney's office, saying, "Hey, do you have a second?" First, It screws up people's productivity, and as a bonus it allows me to get it out when I want and they can receive it when they can.

Inbox by Google is our preferred email tool. (See previous chapter on Inbox Zero).

Zoom for video calls because it's free and you can record every session.

Crowdcast for webinars and our members-only Process Hackers.

Calendly is an essential to scheduling because it allows you to set up your day or week's availability precisely. I give people the link and tell them to book anytime that works for them. However, when they go to my Calendly page, they will never see availability on a Monday. They will never see availability on a Friday. Also, they will never see availability between 3:00 PM and 5:00 PM because that's when I pick up my kids and do after school activities with them. So I have created a corral that I am comfortable with and I know when those things will happen because it is linked to my calendar with its built in notifications.

So next we want to put this into place. Whether you have a team of 2 or 200, planning for scalability requires you having scalable communications.

CHAPTER SIX

PERFECT YOUR PROCESS

Everything we do in our businesses has some level of process to it. The big problem is many people don't tend to study the processes themselves. They go through the motions, and when the process gets too cumbersome, they think, "I need more help."

So they hire more people and throw more people at an inefficient process that doesn't work. If this sounds familiar to you, it's time to look at how we can make processes bulletproof from the start.

Now, many people are going to say, "I don't have time to stop and working on my processes. I'm too busy, or I don't have time to test these things out or experiment with these new tools." It's like saying you don't have time to sleep. I mean you have to sleep.

You also have to put your business under a microscope because like the guy who trained me for my IRONMAN used to say, "The more we sweat in training, the less we will bleed in war."

I assure you there is always a war when it comes to business. Something will come up; something will happen. Things will go wrong, and people will quit. When your "irreplaceable" team members leave, your business will stall. I have seen companies, time and time again, that have ultimately failed because they didn't put proper processes in place. I don't want to see that happen to you.

At the end of the chapter, you will be able to optimize any process by breaking it down into steps, identifying and eliminating redundancy which makes the process as efficient as possible.

So what exactly does it means to optimize and why is it first in the OAO Methodology? It's simple. We can not expect to take an inefficient process, give it to somebody else or throw in some pieces of software and then have it become magically more efficient. It just does not and will not happen. Optimizing means getting you as quickly as possible from start to finish. If it takes 20 minutes to go from point A to point B and you can turn that into 10 minutes by making the process more efficient, that's a pretty significant savings regarding time and money. (Not to mention the rush of dopamine you'll get from accomplishing the task well and in record time!)

Seven years ago, I was using a virtual assistant based in India. Her name was Christine. She and I worked together for over a year. She was awesome. One day she called me and said, "I'm so excited and so sad at the same time." I said, "Why? What's wrong? She said, "I'm being promoted to a manager at the company, which is great, but they won't let me be an assistant anymore. I can't work for you anymore." The blood rushed to my face, "Well what do we do? What are we going to do?

I had a panic attack. Then I asked Christine to do me a favor and write out everything she did for me on a regular basis. Now she had been working for me for a year and a half, and I quite honestly had forgotten. After two days, she sent me a list of 50 things. I looked at it, and right away I thought, "Gosh, I don't even need her to do 15 of those things anymore. They don't matter anymore." Then there were another ten things that could quickly be done with software that wasn't available the year prior.

It was for two reasons. First, I had no idea how long Christine had been going through the motions without any oversight. Second, I didn't know what was involved in my daily processes. So we must begin asking questions like, "Why are we doing things the way we're doing it," what are the steps involved?

Break it down step by step, and once we get that process optimized, we can look at automation and outsourcing. The actions taken to complete a process may be limited, but we must memorialize every one of them in detail.

How do we do it?

Well optimizing the process can be tedious and time-consuming, but as I said before, "the more we sweat in training, the less we bleed in war." Preparation is what we need to grow well, but it requires you to pause and reflect, which is not an entrepreneur's "happy place." Still, if you think ahead, not only will you avoid errors, but you'll be able to see the future of your business where things might be heading. There are parts of processes that you can optimize now, but in the future, something may help you take it even further along. Not knowing what "it" is, makes it impossible to know what "it" could be. Do the work now.

I'm particularly proud of my podcast process. When I started my podcast six years ago, I was doing all the work myself which was about 15 hours per episode. I was doing all the audio editing; I was doing the graphics work, the social media, the transcriptions, everything. Not only was I doing it all myself, but I wasn't good at any of it, so it was taking me twice as long to do it as somebody who knew what the heck they were doing.

I only wanted to do the interviews. At the time there were no services that I knew of that could help. So I had to build it. Now, I knew I needed to have the audio edited. I wanted to have a transcript. I wanted to have show notes. I wanted to put it on Youtube. I wanted to follow up with the guests. Those were my pieces of the process. Now I had to create the glue; the automation. I needed to set up the first domino that would be my recorded audio saved in Dropbox.

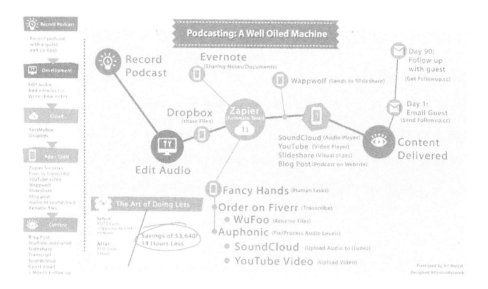

Now, this documentation is a little out of date. In fact, it's quite tricky to write a book about processes and automation, because new technology arrives on a weekly basis. However, the illustration gives you a chance to see all the particulars involved.

First, we look at the major components. So there's record, audio, edit audio, do transcription, post to social media. The lines between them are the automation.

The audio gets edited using Fiverr.

I save it to Dropbox.

It triggers Zapier to send content to Evernote.

Evernote sends show notes to Fancy Hands.

Fancy Hands does time stamps and uploads podcast to iTunes and YouTube.

Also, I wanted it to go on our blog, and I wanted to follow up via email with the guests. First, on the day the podcast aired; and then 90 days later, to check in using Followup cc. Well it was all running pretty smoothly, but I kept running into a problem in the process, and that was that I would always have a different person on Fiverr do the audio editing.

So what I did was tell Fancy Hands to go on Fiverr and find someone who does audio for this amount of money, and there were dozens. I gave them this file with instructions. I purposely wanted it done by different people every time including Fancy Hands. Fancy Hands was an on-demand service so I could record podcasts in one day and have four of these processes running concurrently.

The problem I was running into is that the instructions for Fancy Hands to give to Fiverr were, "edit this audio and when completed rename the file -- first and last name of the guest, the guest date and then save it to this dropbox."

Almost every single time that part of the process would get messed up because they would rename it whatever they wanted. They didn't pay attention to those instructions. So that's when I started using electronic forms. I learned that if you uncover an inefficiency, you can add in a process to make it more fail-safe.

The Japanese refer to as a Poka-yoke. It's something that was created in Toyota manufacturing decades ago, and mainly it's a cog that is put into a task that slows it down technically, but also makes it so you cannot move beyond that point if the work is not done correctly. By putting a form in place like Wufoo or Jotform, you require the person working on that part of the process to complete it the way you want it; otherwise the form cannot be submitted.

There was no way it could be messed up unless somebody purposely put in information incorrectly and there wasn't much we could do about that. It was eye-opening for me for two reasons. First, the idea of putting in a stop, because the pause made the process more efficient. Second, if I hadn't gone through this process first, I wouldn't have been able to see those little intricacies and fix it from the start.

When thinking about a process, ask these questions. Get as granular as you can.

> What does it break down into?

> What are the different phases?

What steps do you take in each phase?

What are the things that have to be completed before the next thing that happened?

Then we want to make a screencast of you performing the process. So if this is a computer-based process, it's straightforward. You can use iCloud or Loom. Now do it as inefficiently as possible. Don't do it in a way that you think is what somebody needs to hear it. Just talk through how you do it. Click around, make mistakes. Show it. Don't tell it. Teaching is not the same thing as showing when we are dealing with processes. Ask the person to make a checklist of the process they just viewed. Then give it to a third person to go through the process and see if they can replicate it. There's no way. Mistakes will come up. Somebody going through can say, "All right, well I didn't understand what you meant at section one?"

Many people when they make processes, they write them out. They refer to assets in apps in relative terms instead of absolute terms. For example,

The first step might be,

"Open the payroll documents."

"Well, where is the payroll document?

"How do I access it?"

"Do I need a password or username?"

...all too relative.

Speak in absolute terms.

"Go to the payroll document. Here is the link to it."

"The username and password are in your password manager under "payroll"

The other thing that people tend to do is use relative terms when referring to people. So you might see a process that says, "When you're done with this, send it to Sarah for review". It's relative. It should say, "When you're done with this, send it to the HR Director for review."

It's then not dependent on a specific person knowing a particular thing. The information contained within the process is documented and easily accessible to everyone.

So that's how you build a fireproof process. The goal should be that you could literally grab somebody off the street and bring him in and he could do the process for you seamlessly.

If you can get there, you'll never be beholden to somebody again. Sarah can be sick. Jack can be out on family leave. The bottleneck breaks. When you perfect your process, you've taken a decisive step toward becoming deliriously replaceable.

It feels good right?

CHAPTER SEVEN

IDEA TO ACHIEVEMENT

I want you to be able to identify the people and resources you need to turn your ideas for your business into reality. My friend, Dan Sullivan, loves to talk about how a lot of people get stuck in the "how" when they're running their business. "How do I get this thing done? How do I do this?" But as Dan says, what they need to be thinking about is "Who." By that, he means surrounding yourself with people who allow you to become more replaceable.

By the way, I'm the who that can tell you how.

So let's go over the basics of project management; how you're going to take those captured ideas and those optimized processes and determine what's going to happen next. Most importantly, who is going to help make those things a reality?

We'll be looking at identifying the problem rather than the solution. I realize this may run counter to your, "get it done, glass half full, live in the solution" mindset, but it's a mistake. Many founders make it, and I don't want you to be one of them.

Project management is not a To-Do List. To-Do lists lack velocity. The typical list has tasks on it that you cannot do right now. They are either too grand, or it's out of your control, for instance, waiting on somebody else, but they're all commingled in one place.

"Get dry cleaning" and "Write Book," do not belong in the same place.

It's our job to retrain our brains when it comes to to-do lists because we are not wired for a higher level of compartmentalization. It's called the Zeigarnik effect; where people remember uncompleted or interrupted tasks better than completed tasks. It's the voice in our heads that pushes us to complete the uncompleted; the items on our To-Do list. But we also have this thing called cognitive dissonance which is psychological stress that occurs when we hold two or more contradictory beliefs, ideas or values simultaneously. We push to get it done; we can't get it done. We can't move forward; we desperately want to move forward. So we make more lists about the lists, on whiteboards, in journals, with apps and all of these methods serve to make us less productive.

If we can think about velocity and the phases of those projects, we can break the loggerhead. If we get a task, understand what it entails by breaking it down into components, then hand off bits and parts of it as quickly as possible, we are gaining momentum.

Newton's First Law of Motion, the law of inertia, states, "An object at rest stays at rest, and an object in motion stays in motion with the same speed and the same direction unless acted upon by an unbalanced force."

My goal is to get you to relinquish your role as "the unbalanced force." If you are the one to do it, terrific! But you shouldn't be holding anybody up in the process.

A project in motion should be built up of tasks. How are we moving things from one phase to the next? What are those phases? It can be as simple as "to do, doing, and done" which is a typical arc of any Kanban view in Trello, for example. The project could have 20 phases to it, but the point is that there is movement. We know what's on deck, what's being worked on now and what's complete.

Here's the crux of project management and the mistake too many founders make. Far too often people come to me with the solution rather than the problem. It's one of the things that differentiates leaders; their ability to identify problems faster. If you can tie solutions to them; great. Or if you know the person who has a solution that's also great. But think about the situations in your life and your business where you have struggled and stagnated with a possible solution before ever stating the problem. It's a "cart before the horse" perspective that makes project management impossible.

For example, somebody asked me recently,

"What's the best CRM these days?"

They, of course, are expecting me to answer, XY CRM or AB CRM.

But I don't.

I say, "Why do you need a CRM?"

And they respond, "Well, I just heard about this one that my competitor was using, or I was at a conference, and they showed this CRM, and it looked cool. Or the best one is, Well there was an incredible deal on it".

For most people, the real problem is terrible customer service, and they think a CRM will cure it. But that's not true. You could do it with CRM, but that's not the solution. The solution is developing a process for better follow up, and the answer is probably internal rather than a shiny external solution, that isn't going to solve the embedded problem.

I use the RACI model a lot in project management discussions. It stands for

Responsible

Accountable

Consulted

Informed.

The responsible person is the person who has to sign off on it. Often you, the founder, will be the responsible person. The accountable person is the one who is going to get it done. Now the founder might have to sign off on it, but the actual work done by someone else.

The consulted person is the one whose help is needed; a specialist for example, who isn't doing the work or signing off on it, merely offering much-needed input. Lastly, the informed person is the one who needs to be made aware of progress or completion. Here is the space I want you to inhabit. So overlay that model on the team you have. Who are the missing people?

Now think about the resources you have.

What technology resources?

What money?

What kind of software do we have available?

What content do we have available?

Who is in our network?

Identify the available resources, both internal and external which will help. These all constitute the systems for success. The tasks associated with the answers to all these project-based questions must be specific and realistic.

For example, If you need to write a 750-word article and it's going to take you three hours to write it, then break down the tasks into fifteen minutes intervals. Outline, research, interviews, first 250 words. Get as microscopic as possible because our limited attention spans demand it. We build momentum and velocity through the achievement of micro-goals, and every successful project is the culmination of many micro-goals.

Another essential element of a project management system is its collaborative nature; putting all the pieces in a setting that makes sense, has flow, and can be replicated by someone other than you.

Ideally, you're using something like Trello or Airtable; you can integrate those resources easily. So if that resource is a person, add them to the board. If it's an automation, you can use the myriad integrations like Zapier. The goal is to provide a level of transparency concerning the stages that a standard To-Do list can never satisfy.

Finally, let's talk about deadlines. "As Soon As Possible" is a phrase founders should erase from their lexicon. It doesn't mean anything, adds a level of stress, and is indicative of poor planning. Rather, get in the habit of establishing artificially restrictive limits on the work. If your project management clearly illustrates when it's needed, ASAP is futile. Specifically, establish when you need it. Don't say, "We could do it tomorrow." Make it, tomorrow. Make the deadline and if necessary, work backward from it to figure out what steps need to take in place to get you to that deadline.

Under promise and over deliver. There shouldn't be soft deadlines. When we restrict ourselves to deadlines and processes, we enjoy a paradoxical feeling of liberation.

CHAPTER EIGHT

JUSTIN KAVANAUGH - THE SULTAN OF SPEED

*For roughly 15 years I've said and done the same thing.
It's worked remarkably well. There's data. My training
methods work. My athletes achieve incredible things. I
run the best speed institute, hands down. However, that
mindset was not helping me in my business or my life. I
had some huge revelations about how I ran my
business, and now, a year later, I am no longer as
involved in the task-oriented part of the company.*

I am now completely focused on the strategy and the outcome of the
business. I have made myself replaceable. I learned how to trust the

process, trust myself and believe others. Oh, and I had to slow down. For a speed coach, that was torture.

Here's what I discovered.

For me the secret sauce, the answer to the question, "How do I stop doing everything when I'm the only person I trust?" was a painful but necessary mindset shift. If you don't trust anyone, you are putting a lid on your opportunities. The hard truth is that most times when people say they don't trust other people to do something, it's just that they don't trust themselves to manage the process.

It's difficult to describe the way something should be done and a lot of people secretly know that they are not as good as they think they are at the process and they're worried that someone else is going to do it better than them or they're concerned about being judged for their inability to articulate the tasks needed to achieve a certain level of competency. They worry too much about how they will be judged, both externally and internally. That mindset creates procrastination, an internal struggle that has a huge effect on external output.

Here's what happened...

Two seasons of the year, I was entirely focused on training and being in the business as a technician and working on it and I liked that... my NFL program, my pro athlete training program our summer training programs. Then during the other two seasons, fall and spring, our coaches ran the business. So I thought that I was almost there and I felt that I was in balance with what I wanted.

However, I had completely misinterpreted the role of a CEO and the idea of taking ownership. It became extreme ownership where I thought I was responsible for everything. But I was creating chaos, creating problems. I was making bottlenecks to feel important. It was so unproductive.

So my days during the offseason, our business was great. I worked on the strategy for my brand. I worked on building the infrastructure of the company and then during the busy seasons I was knee deep and nowhere to be found other than working IN the business. It became overwhelming because I knew I wanted to get out of that day in day world and spend all my time in the world where I could take it to another level. I wasn't able to do that full time. Ultimately it became obvious that if you took me out of the equation. It didn't work in the busiest times of the year, but with me it was great.

So why didn't it work?

Well, the skills I have and have been selling for so long are so high that training somebody else to do it would take years, not months. So that was out. It then became a question of onboarding talent because I finally let go of the idea that I was the only one who knew how to train elite athletes the way I do. I needed a better system to find these people. It forced me to articulate the what, the why, and how, so then I could determine the who. Ari asked me when I worked with him in New York last year, "What was your plan, from the business standpoint. I said, "We were executing it. We were doing it. He said, "Well, what changed?"

Well, my wife and I had gotten on the same page about our careers. It wasn't easy to do, but we agreed that she was going to pursue her career in the corporate world of finance and I was going to continue an entrepreneurial path.

So we decided on the direction that we were headed. I was going to be traveling. I was going to build my brand and speak and get those things going. We went on vacation and locked it in. My wife accepted a job that was going to be about 30 percent travel and I took speaking opportunities across the globe. Then when they got back, she accepted the job opportunity and then pretty soon after we got home, we found out that she was pregnant. So she had to rescind the offer.

Now, many people might look at it as the arrow in the heart of your career, but we took it on as an opportunity. She was going to make the short-term sacrifices for family, and I needed to do something to get myself removed from the actual day to day. I couldn't travel anymore for two to three weeks at a time because I wanted to be at home with my family and be there for her. So, that's where Ari came into the picture. I remember, all I asked him was, "How do I automate this?" I wanted to automate everything. But what I found is I needed to optimize the process before I could automate anything.

I think that was one of the most significant Aha moments for me. I had to do the hardest thing for me in my career at that time, and that was to say no to people that I had already said yes. I was backing down from my word because I had already committed to speaking engagements and that was during the time my son was supposed to be born. I couldn't be out of the country. So I had to tell people in organizations that committed to me that I couldn't do it anymore.

It was hard because I was always somebody that said I had to say yes to everything. I had to align my decisions with my priorities before they became too much to handle. I was in a corner, I had no choice, so like a boxer, it was either get punched in the face or block and pivot or jab out of it.

However, sometimes we drop our hands and then we're more vulnerable, but if you never find yourself in those situations, you never learn to make a better decision. So I had to learn to say no, an idea that runs counter to my character, opened up a whole new way of thinking and approaching my life and my business.

Look, I'm one of the top speed coaches in the world, and I've trained some of the fastest athletes in sport. But what I learned, the value I've gotten from making myself replaceable is that sometimes going slow is the only way to solve a problem. For me to become faster and better I had to slow down the process, look at what and why I was doing what I was doing, and build it back up.

It was the most painful thing I've ever done. As an entrepreneur, you want to move fast as a high performer, whether it be in sport or business as a C level executives right?. A business owner wants to move quickly because stagnation kills people. Right? The one thing that you want to do is be excited about what's new and what's coming next. The last thing you want to do is be stuck.

When you stop, that's where you can make the most significant change. That's where you're in the corner, and you have to make a move. So when you force yourself to be in that position, you allow yourself to be proactive instead of reactive. It's counterintuitive, but it works.

If you're moving fast, the faster you're going to fix things on the fly, you don't ever stop and say, okay, we need to slow this down to get it right. The answer in most cases from your employees and from the people who work with you is, "well, that's the way it's always been done."

That is the scariest thing to hear in business because that's not going to get you to the next level. When you're working with athletes, and they move up from one level to the next, there's a particular skill set that got them there. Often they forget that, and they work on something else, but then they lose their foundation. However, the more significant problem is that they think what gets them from point A to point B is the same thing that gets them from point B to point C. It's not. No way.

It was not only limiting beliefs, but my attachment to the process. I say to my athletes all the time, I am agnostic about the process, but I'm religious to the results. Whatever we used to get us there, as long as that is ethically sound and it is in line with our values, I am okay with doing it. So I'm not willing to take a shortcut to get us to the result, but I'm definitely interested in getting us there faster and quicker by using a more optimized process. It was crazy that I was using that in my training philosophy, but I wasn't using that in my business. It was the most significant pivotal moment for me that someone (Ari) treated me like an athlete from a business standpoint.

I was able to put my faith in him. I trusted him. He was speaking a language I understood because I use it all the time. I believe you should meet people where they are as an athlete to get them to work, to get them where they want to be. You got to figure that out. Ari was basically the key to the handcuffs to get us out of that mindset because he was giving us contextual solutions. He saw where we were and knew how to get us where we wanted to go.

Specifically, I need to operate with Level Five Delegation to be productive. It is the most productive zone for me where I know there's trust but things need to be verified. I used to like to create chaos because it made me feel important. I could fix it. Now I just tell myself, I've taught my team to think better and problem solve. Let it go. So anytime that there's a problem in the business, it's a good thing now because we understand that it probably is not going to come up multiple times, and if it does, we are the problem.

We have to take the time to think about these things because these things are essential and if you don't take the time to think about whether your ego is the only thing that's important and that there's a solution to getting out of your way, then nothing gets done. There are all kinds of things that we can show people how to do, but unless we have that initial change in perspective, then you're not willing to change anything if you're not willing to say, I need help. I'm the bottleneck. Fundamentally, I want it yesterday. I'm the best person for the job. I got this. But If you're not willing to look at the destructive nature of those phrases, then your business isn't going to go anywhere. I mean, it'll go someplace, but you're going to hate your life. When you have this roadmap laid out for you, it flows better; the resistance disappears because you've already decided that you're amenable to seeing the world differently.

CHAPTER NINE

THE SIX LEVELS OF DELEGATION

One of my goals is to help you delegate paths with efficiency, effectiveness, and confidence. If we follow the OAO Methodology sequentially, and we've arrived at the outsourcing part, then we're poised for success. But we have to learn how to delegate properly first.

There are so many activities that you're doing that you should not be doing; and while that may seem obvious, we tend to lose sight of this notion. Delegation is too often the first line of defense for founders and it really should be the last line.

I'm going to steal an exercise from Dan Sullivan (again) to illustrate the point. It called the ABC's and Unique Ability®.

As a founder you engage in three activities, A, B and C. A is the thing you are excellent at; you are absolutely the best in your work here. We all have some sort of unique ability and whether we're using it or not is not relevant. It is a gift you possess. You could be excellent at organizational methods, you could be excellent at crunching numbers, you could be a gifted communicator.

B, the second tier, is where you are competent, but you're not passionate. C is things that you are not very good at all, but you do them anyway.

Now, I'm not judging, but columns B and C are the tasks we need to stop doing. We need to focus and organize ourselves in a way that ultimately allows us to apply our best abilities to the places that can receive the most significant benefit.

For example, accounting. People who excel here love organization. They like to start and finish something concrete like a balance sheet or projection. I admire that kind of attention to detail, but this work would not only drive me crazy, but I'd be terrible at it. I'm just not wired that way. So I don't do it. I delegate it to people who are adroit and passionate about the pursuit.

Once we have determined our ABCs, we can start to unburden ourselves from a multitude of work. However, we need an organized philosophy and system in place. So it all begins with our ego. Better yet, the relinquishing of the idea, that "You got it." You don't, and unproductive self-reliance is no longer serving a purpose.

However, when we delegate, we are empowering people. It, in turns, enables us to be an even better, more visionary leader.

We are allowing a team and a person to grow by providing them with opportunities that ultimately help drive us forward. Reframe the question, "How do I get ahead?" to "How does my team help me get ahead" to eventually, "How do I help my team get ahead?" It's the sort of arc of that you need to go through when we contemplate proper delegation.

Delegation is by no means, "Just do this thing." Delegation is leadership. It forces you to communicate your vision effectively and your needs so somebody else so that they feel ownership and pride over the work that they do. It allows them to solve problems independently and ultimately your vision can be achieved more effectively.

What are the common pitfalls in delegation? The biggest one in my experience has been that founders use it as the first line of defense. "Just get this done." However, if you don't optimize the process first, it will take them longer to do it. There will be mistakes. In other words, if you make an inefficient process and give it to somebody else who has even less context than you do, the odds of it becoming more efficient are very unlikely.

The automation step is critical to delegation as well. Never imagine that an app or platform or software program will work for a human who does not take ownership of it. Throwing automated solutions at team members without optimized processes means that someone's desktop will be littered with unused icons collecting virtual dust. A founder may think that Intercom is the panacea for all that ails her organization. However, if she doesn't optimize the process and engage her team, there will be no progress.

When systems and processes are firmly in place, a founder is ready to jump into outsourcing; the last line of defense. The bonus of using this approach is that you are adding value to the process.

Still, I get my fair share of pushback on the delegation component. My favorite being, "Nobody can do this as well as I can." To whit, I usually reply, "BS, you are not the best at everything. You are probably not the best at more than three things. So it's a sign of strength, not weakness to admit it."

There's always going to be somebody who might be able to do it better and faster than you. It also doesn't matter if you can get it done more quickly. Even if it takes you one minute, that one minute pulls you out of your ability to be in a flow state for 20 minutes or more and research supports my observation.

Generally speaking, for every minute of traffic stoppage because of an accident or road work, it takes approximately 43 minutes for traffic patterns to return to normal. So if the traffic stops for 10 minutes, it's going to take upwards of six hours for that traffic pattern to return to normal. It's the same thing with our brains. Remember that there is a big difference between how long it takes you to get something done versus how long it takes you to do it. Now it might only take you a minute, but if distractions make it impossible for you to get to it for two days, how productive are you being?

Then I usually hear founders ask, "What if it doesn't get done?" It's where the six levels of delegation come into play; which is a framework for deciding how we think through what we delegate, to whom we delegate, and what information we need to give them.

So start with something small and work your way up. You can build in stop gaps and checks to make sure that the processes don't get screwed up. Ultimately, it's a matter of trust, and trust like coral takes a long time to grow and is very easy to break; which is why so many of us have trouble with it.

Maybe you don't trust them with the information. You don't want to give someone your passwords or your social security number. However, the truth of the matter is that there are enough protections in place for the average person out there that's it's not a significant concern. Also, if anybody wants to information, they're going to get it.

However, the other side of the trust issue refers back to the first question, which is that you don't trust that somebody can do it. I'm a control freak.

It's true for many entrepreneurs, but that doesn't help make you a better leader. Management is not the same as leadership management. Authority and leadership are not the same things because there are many people in positions of authority who are not leaders and then there are leaders who do not command authority. In my business, I am the leader of the team, but they can say no to my ideas. They can veto me. I am not and don't want to be the authority on all things.

So here's a quick story about a bad outsourcing experience I had. I used to get many parking tickets in New York City. I've always had commercial vehicles for most of my adult life. I was working in construction and real estate, so I had pickup trucks, hybrid cars, but all of them were commercial. Now in New York City, it's challenging to park, but the law would say a commercial vehicle can load and unload.

However, I would still get tickets and would have to write in and show a receipt or an invoice to the effect that you were making some delivery. So I automated this process using a virtual assistant company in India. The ticket would come up. They would modify an invoice, send it in, and show that I was legitimately in and out all day.

They would mail it in and 90 percent of the time I'd get the tickets thrown out.

I did that for several years and then a couple of years ago I got a big package in the mail from the New York Department of Finance. They were questioning the validity of many of my reversals. It ended up being many, many thousands of dollars in fines because the VA service kept sending the same invoice over and over and I never checked. Trying to explain what a virtual assistant was to a judge in a New York City court was not very successful. It was a painful and expensive lesson, but it was an excellent example of the mistakes you can make if you outsource before you optimize.

Still, the onus is on you to flex your delegation muscle. You will make mistakes, and you will learn from them, and you will improve. The more that you do, the more time you will enjoy to do what YOU do best, and your team will benefit as well.

People are hesitant to employ the six levels of delegation because they see it as a binary activity. Either I'm keeping everything to myself, or I'm giving everything away, and most people are not comfortable giving everything away. So recognizing that there are these several levels that are valid at different stages, for various tasks is crucial.

The first one is, "Do as I say." It's pretty basic. For example, "Buy this book on Amazon." "What time is the next train to Rhinebeck?"

The second level is, "Look into this." Here is where you start to ask for someone's opinion. "I need a flight from Phoenix to New York on this date. Find me some options, look into it." So they're going to look into it, and come back with what they found. Usually, with Level 2, you are merely delaying the inevitable. You probably could have done this kind of work yourself unless it's something specialized.

Level Three is, "Give me your advice and I'll decide." It is a pivotal one because this is where you start to allow people to make some decisions. A good example here would be a research project "Give me two options. Find me the top 10 real estate brokers in the Miami area. Come back to me with the results and your method."

Level Four is the next step in independent decision-making. You want to hire a funnel specialist but don't know anything about funnels. Ask a team member to find the best people at the right price and decide who would do the best job for your organization. Ask to be given the name of the person she agreed upon.

Level five, and level six are my favorites. Level five is one that many people never think about if they're not familiar with outsourcing. It's defined as, "Explore and decide within these limits." You're telling people when not to contact you, and this is very empowering because you're telling them you can go from here to here to here too and I don't need to know about it. Don't wait for me.

Finally, level six. "Take care of it." Say I want to set up a Webinar next week. I don't know about it until it's scheduled. Do the slides. Do the marketing, the Facebook ads, the setup, everything. The typical thing we do in my team is a hybrid between five and six, which is level six with a timeframe.

So if somebody asks me for my input on something on the team, they know that if I don't get back to them in an hour, they should go. Now that requires an enormous amount of trust and outstanding people.

Now, by the way, this may seem superfluous to say that tasks need to be within budget, which is your job to enumerate.

Finally, there's internal versus external delegation. Internally, stick to your column A tasks. Use people you have on your team to do the B tasks. Outsource externally as much as you can from the C column to the two different kinds of virtual assistant model; which are "on demand' and "dedicated." So dedicated is pretty apparent. It's where you have contact with the same person every day, enabling you to build a relationship and ultimately allow this person to be a forward facing addition to your brand.

The demand model is where you have access to dozens, maybe hundreds, maybe thousands of virtual assistants. They tend to be cheaper, more available, with quick response time, and a wider variety of skills. However, it's difficult to use these services for big tasks, because there is no continuity.

If you are dipping your toes into the outsourcing waters, start with an on-demand service so you can practice communicating your optimized process. Use it to fix the potholes in your systems and to find a rhythm that works for you. We have then arrived at the part where feeling replaceable is going to start to feel incredible!

CHAPTER TEN

HIRING AND ONBOARDING

Automating your hiring process will grow your team and business with a minimal amount of hands-on work. Today the process is not a generic assembly line where people come to you, you process them in a particular way and put them in a system of sorts. Understanding that you can achieve a seamless flow in all aspects of your business using hiring as an example will supercharge your productivity and those of the team around you.

So let's first go through the good, the bad, and the ugly in the hiring process. It can be a nasty experience for many companies because there is so much at risk and a bad hire can be one of the most expensive things a business absorbs. There's the time spent and lost, and you will probably miss out on client work if you have to redouble your internal efforts.

First ask yourself, "What do you actually want?" Yes, you want to hire outstanding people consistently, have them fit the culture, and help drive your company forward. However, what do you really want? Well, it starts by looking at the people that you already have on the team. If you don't have a team, you have to uncover the skill sets you need.

Importantly, hiring needs to be something that has nothing to do with one person. It can't be like betting on horses. So look at the skill sets that you have in place now.

Remember *the Peter Principle*? It says that people get promoted to the point of obsolescence. If you promote people based on their current performance, they will get to a point where they're no longer effective. So we want to avoid that.

Focus your searches on skill sets, rather than people and the problem disappears. I look at three skill sets that are innate to a person, so they can't become obsolete, they move into another set of skills. One is proactivity. I want somebody to be proactive. Ask somebody to order something for you. Everyone can do that. The proactive person says, "I'm going to follow up to make sure that it got delivered or I'm going to follow up and make sure that they were happy with it." That's productivity. I don't think you can train that in people. You can put it in any process that you like, and it might get done, but you're not going to instill productivity in somebody else.

Second is attention to detail. I don't have it, but it's something I require the people that I work with to have because they catch the mistakes, correct the grammar, and see that this person's name isn't on the list and they're coming to this event. Again, I don't think that's trainable.

The final skill is curiosity; people who are thirsty to learn new things. If you look at the most successful people in the world, they're always learning. I think Warren Buffett and Bill Gates spend about 80 percent of their day reading. I want to surround myself with people who want to learn. I never want people on the team or working with me, who are complacent.

Next, we have to attract candidates. Present yourself in your hiring process as you would to your customers. You wouldn't take two weeks to respond to a client, don't do it to candidates. It makes you look like a disorganized company, and you may lose solid prospects.

Almost all aspects of the hiring process can be automated. From the posting to the onboarding, so there is no reason for inefficiency here. When I was hiring at a virtual assistant company I co-founded, we employed 183 high-quality people in 16 months, who worked in 17 different time zones.

It was and is a very scalable process. The key to its success is to be clear about what the candidate will be doing, not necessarily who they are or where they went to school. Will they be supporting the founder of the company to impart vision through content creation? Will they be ensuring the financial stability of the organization? Exploring new programs and markets?

Now the application. There is an enormous number of websites that will help you with job postings. I'm not going to help you with that. However, here's a great hack for navigating the application process itself. Think about how you can put somebody in a situation where you can watch them do something poorly rather than letting them do well. Why? Because there's a lot more to be gained by watching someone to do something poorly, then watching, them do it the right way. For example, never ask somebody to create something for an application. Ask them to fix something.

If you're hiring writers, never ask them to submit samples of their work. It's a terrible idea. Firstly, you don't know if it took them six months to craft that one, 500-word blog post. You don't even know if they wrote it. Instead, give them a poorly written blog post and ask them to make it better. Don't ask somebody to create a WordPress site for you or take this one-pager and make a PayPal button. Instead, put a PayPal button on it that doesn't work and ask them to fix it.

Next, see how they behave in an uncomfortable situation. We used to ask applicants to make a three minute YouTube video of themselves, saying why they wanted to work for our company. We were able to use that as a litmus test. Ten percent of the people couldn't figure out how to upload a YouTube video. So for our purposes, it acted as an immediate weed-out. Also, if they're not comfortable in their own home, on camera, they're not going to be comfortable with other people necessarily or with clients.

What follows is a hiring task we used that worked beautifully.

We said a client was staying at a specific hotel in Texas. He had a thousand envelopes stamped with first-class stamps that he needed to mail. We asked them to find the nearest place to send them; ideally something within walking distance.

Several people would say, "The nearest post office is three point two miles away. It's a 45-minute walk," or they'd say, "I'll look into that and get right back to you." Neither answer was what we were looking for at all. The right answer belonged to the person who called the hotel, spoke to the concierge who told them that there is a FedEx office on site. They called the FedEx office to confirm that they could accept the envelopes and some folks even reported back that the hotel would collect them from the client's room. When you test for proactivity, the results are quite visible.

Once you've whittled down your candidates, automations are going to speed up the rest of the process. You can have background checks, contract signings, internal documentation all integrated with Zapier, so you know at a glance where a candidate is in the hiring process and what exactly are the missing pieces.

Then integrate your company's internal and external communication systems with the hiring process, and you are now testing a candidate's ability to work with the structures you have in place.

We use Trello for project management and Slack for internal communication. Our candidates access a dummy system that allows us to see how facile they are with our processes.

Final "face-to-face" interviews can be very efficient if you limit the time to ten minutes and the questions to four. Make the first two questions, softballs, and the second two, hardballs. The first question, "Why you?" Second question, "Why us?" The third question, "Tell me about a time you messed up at work and how did you handle it?" The fourth question is my favorite interview question of all time. 'If we don't hire you, why do you think that will be?"

So my answer to that question would have been, "Well, I probably present myself as a bit of a lone wolf and I do work well by myself. But the truth is that I'm actually a really good team player. I'm just a little awkward at first." My advice would be to look for people who know themselves, are not afraid to be honest and can deal with an awkward situation with grace.

Automations speed up the onboarding process as well if you have a process in place for bringing folks into your organization. The training process was as much a learning process for us concerning how to train new hires as it was for them. However, once we had a system in place, through trial and error, we could get people up to speed in record time.

We added an offboarding step which also proved invaluable. It would trigger a manager to remove them from all the systems before an email from us informing them that they were let go. It streamlined the process, protected our clients and our proprietary assets.

To the reader: should you be interested in replicating this process, the details regarding the automations we used and the sequences we built can be found on my Medium blog: *https://medium.com/less-doing/how-we-automated-our-hiring-process-in-3-hours*

CHAPTER ELEVEN

CONTENT CREATION

Content is king. I don't care what business you're in, whether you are a plumber or an accountant or a neurosurgeon, content is the secret sauce. The good news is, we are all creative because the ability, actually the need, to make ourselves heard, is part of the human experience.

We are all storytellers to a degree, and if we seek to make lasting connections, we need to share our experiences with the world. So we're not only talking about how you can create content but also how to hang it out there and how you can plan it and produce it efficiently.

Your voice and your content are unique, and you can leverage it with great success. Generally speaking, there are three audiences for your content. You should rarely be creating content that serves one audience. Be in the mindset of:

What other ways can I get this message out?

Who else should see this?

Where else would this be beneficial?

The big ideas you have swirling around your head also take away from your ability to think of other things. So, let's optimize them because our intellectual property is an irreplaceable commodity. Creating and disseminating content correctly and effectively will make you competitive and innovative, and you don't need many resources.

Many people say, "Nobody cares about what I do. It can be really boring." Well, that's just not true. There are many things we take for granted in our daily lives that other people could find not only informative but transformative. We have to deliver the information and watch it turn into wisdom. Once someone has received your knowledge, you have a raving fan.

My pal Joe Polish says, "People won't buy from you because they understand you. They buy from you because they feel understood." It's a subtle difference, for sure. Content is the way to build that empathy.

Good content also pays enormous dividends regarding lead generation. So we want to spend as little time as possible creating it so we can capitalize on the leads it generates. Podcasts have been an excellent source of lead generation for me. However, it's not for everybody. There's a particular demographic that adores podcasts and others who have never even listened to one. My audience loves podcasts. Some people are not fans of reading, don't approach them through blog posts. Some people do not want to consume video content, stay away from YouTube videos. Know your audience before embarking on your content plan, and you will save a lot of time.

Next, determine how often you want to publish, the schedule is entirely up to you and doesn't have to be a daily thing, but stay consistent.

I write an article once a week. I do a webinar once a month. I podcast twice a month. I send out email newsletters twice a week. Social media four times a week. What can you handle? What does your audience want? Do you get pushback on the volume of content you send your list? Then ease up and find another avenue.

When scheduling, try to pick thematic structures that are evergreen. In other words, take the foundational pillars of your organization and organize content around them that can be reused and published over time. For example, if you are in Wealth Management, use the monthly or bi-monthly pillars of Financial Freedom, Tax Planning, Student Loans and Retirement. Now drill down on each component to develop content for each. Your audience will start to expect things at certain times, and they'll be prepared mentally for it; so they are more likely to consume it.

If you have followed my previous advice about idea capture, you now have plenty of things to share with your audience. It could be a product, a revelation, a customer experience that was instructive. However, now it's time to develop those ideas further through an avenue with which you are comfortable. If you are not a talker, don't do a podcast or Facebook Live. If you like to write, then craft blog posts for Medium and outsource your ideas to a professional who can write.

I haven't written a blog post for Less Doing in the last ten months. It's been incredibly liberating because I have ideas all the time. I had 60 things that I wanted to write about, but nothing was converting. I was the bottleneck. Also, since, I wanted to write this book, I had to free up some space in my head to dedicate to it.

So we hired a writer who gets me, knows my voice, knows the team and what we're trying to accomplish. I've successfully outsourced this enormous part of my work. Now the system is so efficient; those brainstorms get made into blog posts, which get repurposed on social media platforms and turned into videos at a speed and quality I could not do myself.

I spoke in a previous chapter about my podcast production, but it bears repeating here.

It was taking me about 15 hours per episode to get it done. It was an enormous problem and waste of money because I was putting a new episode out every six weeks and with that schedule, I was not growing a massive following.

So I created this process with the goal in mind of only doing what I do well; which was the recorded interview. I saved the recording into Dropbox, it would go to an audio editor who would add the intro and outro that would go to a show notes writer. Then it would go into to Zapier which would take it to Fancy Hands (at the time,) who would have the audio editing done and publish it.

It would automatically go to SoundCloud and YouTube, and then we would share it on Slideshare and make a blog post out of it from the transcript. Eventually, the guests were emailed the link to share with their audience.

So primarily from one piece of content, we were able to get a blog post, several emails, a lot of social media. The transcription service we use, Temi.com has been outstanding. It takes minutes, and it's like a $1.30 to transcribe it. It's incredible raw material for repurposing, and we use it to its best advantage.

Realistically you could block out an entire day and create the raw material for content for a whole month, using video, audio, a voice message, or a Facebook Live. The next step is to automate as much as possible by getting a service like Temi.com to transcribe everything. Now you have the makings of blog posts, Lumen5 videos, and social media posts that can be outsourced to a writer on your team, or a writing service like Contentfly. Social media posting services abound these days, but I like MeetEdgar because its dashboard is intuitive, easy to navigate and it will also pull in RSS feeds of your choosing to bump up your presence in an auxiliary way. So you are not always "selling" something, but letting your followers know what's on your mind.

It's an authentic connection that builds trust and community. It's storytelling at its best.

CHAPTER TWELVE

THE CUSTOMER JOURNEY

The final trail marker on the path to becoming replaceable is getting a solid handle on who your customer is, and where you would like the relationship with them to go. In order to do this, it's necessary to map out what it looks like for somebody to go from being a stranger to your business, to becoming a lead, then a customer and finally, a raving fan. Someone who shouts your name from the rooftops because you've had such an impact on their lives that they can't help but share it...with other strangers who become leads...

The process involves plotting out your customer journey from pre-sale through long-term relationship building and identifying touch points along the way.

So the first thing you want to look at is, "Where are your leads coming from?"

Word of mouth in a referral based business?

Facebook ads?

Social Media presence?

Events?

Once they are a customer,

How are you communicating with them?

How often and for?

What reasons?

The customer journey is the process by which qualified leads move through a sales funnel. An essential element here is "qualified," because you might have many leads, but they may not be qualified leads. That's why the customer journey is so crucial, because it allows us to pinpoint our customers along a spectrum to isolate how and where we deliver value.

What does the customer value ladder look like? In our business, we have a free Facebook group, the Less Doing Labs, our paid Academy program, our Optimized Operator course, our Mastermind group, The Less Doing Leaders, and finally, our events. It's a very straightforward path. Someone can and has gone from the free program all the way up through to our mastermind, depending on how much he or she interacts with the program.

In developing your customer journey, think about all the specific pain points and goals of one particular person. It's obvious, that that person won't be unique and that their issues will be shared by many. Don't take a shotgun approach, it should be almost surgical, to provide a seamless experience. So it should be an experience, not just a transaction. When you work on this with your team, include every point where you're a customer comes into contact with your business: a Facebook page, a storefront, phone calls, voicemails, emails, Now sort them into the three phases of any interaction: Before, During and After. Before is everything that happens before they become a customer and that can be a very long journey. However, I was taught and believe in the mentality that no one should be left behind when it comes to your marketing journey. That should always be a place for everybody, even if that person inhabits only your free Facebook group. "During" is the marriage part of the program. Now that your relationship is on another level, how do you interact with your customers when they are customers? The honeymoon phase is over, and now the hard work of nurturing and supporting your customers begins.

"After" is the fork in the road. Your customer is going one way. You are heading another. How you handle this seminal moment may be your most important role as a founder. Saying goodbye isn't easy, but can be done with grace and confidence.

Once you have determined who your customer is and the steps they take on the journey; it's time to produce a lead magnet. Because now you know who they are and where they are, and most importantly where you want them to go.

The lead magnet adds much value to the person getting it. Also, it's something that gives your audience, not just something they want, but something they specifically asked for, turning them almost immediately into a "qualified lead."

We've used an assortment of lead magnets, from the first two chapters of a book to infographics, to blueprints, video courses. It's entirely up to you, but give value immediately, then place the lead on the journey you have already outlined.

Capturing emails through targeted and actionable lead magnets is amazingly cost-efficient, and all you need is the offer and a method of capture, like Intercom. If you speak at events, make your presentation available to any audience member who sends a specific text to Textiful. The request AND the person's email will go right into Intercom for your team to handle the request and trigger an email sequence that gives more information about what we do.

There are many theories about what works best in email sequences, and I'm certainly not the foremost authority. But I do know what works for us. We paint a clear picture up front. It's the same as essays in college. "Tell them what you're gonna tell them, tell them, then tell them what you told them.

First, a welcome email that thanks them for asking for the blueprint, video, infographic, and then gives them the broad strokes. The second email should be a straightforward question. So in our case, it's, "What is your productivity challenge?"

Next, is simple text and the person's name as the subject line. It's an interesting thing is that our brains are so desensitized. Most sales emails at this point, scream, limited time sale, one time only, URGENT, and our minds tend to tune that stuff out. So the more boring we can be, the more real our email seems. It's not a trick because it's, it's just the way the brain works. So what we've found is that if you put the person's first name is the subject line, it works exceptionally well.

Next is the inclusion of a super signature. So it says signed by me and says, PS, whenever you're ready, here are four ways I can help you grow your business.

"Whenever you are ready," uses very targeted and specific language. It says to the person that either they're not ready and the person is going to subconsciously, respond, "Well, you know, I want to be ready, or I'm ready, don't tell me I'm not ready." However, it's also entirely benign at the same time; it's not aggressive; we're just offering help. So here are four ways I can help. Make a few of them free and a few paid programs, furthering the notion that people entering into a relationship with you are going someplace....when they are ready.

Include these four items in a super signature on your email platform; every newsletter, every event announcement. The schedule you pick for emailing your customers is also utterly contingent upon the nature of the relationship you have with them. It also depends on what you do too. If you sell life insurance, you probablytalk to your clients once or twice a year. If you sell razors or hair color, you should be talking to them every week. So it depends on the usability and the frequency of purchase.

Once you have a complete picture of the customer and the journey, automation and outsourcing can take care of the rest. It is that simple and allows you, the founder, the quality time you need to nurture the relationships you and your team have worked so hard to cultivate. In the end, you're just replaceable in the day to day, but your value to your customers on their journey can now be enjoyed much more fully.

Cool right?

CHAPTER THIRTEEN

CONCLUDING THOUGHTS

"A human being should be able to change a diaper, plan an invasion, butcher a hog, conn a ship, design a building, write a sonnet, balance accounts, build a wall, set a bone, comfort the dying, take orders, give orders, cooperate, act alone, solve equations, analyze a new problem, pitch manure, program a computer, cook a tasty meal, fight efficiently, die gallantly. Specialization is for insects."

-Robert A. Heinlein, from Time Enough for Love:
Notebooks of Lazarus Long

I love this quote for many reasons, but mostly because it's talking about skills as well as attitudes. It also speaks to my quest for self-sufficiency, agility and becoming more adaptable.

While there are benefits and value to people, who can specialize in things, as entrepreneurs and founders, many times that can be a disadvantage. The truth is if somebody is genuinely specialized, it becomes a lot harder for them to collaborate. There's less they can contribute to somebody else's work and unless they can fully participate, ideas can't be exchanged and propagated.

Replaceable founders can't be too tied to any idea. Imagine a chessboard and any one of us is the king, you can move one space in any direction, including back to where you started. However, that's all you can do. You have to leap and take advantage of opportunities, seize those opportunities and drive people forward. Lead and follow. I think what makes the Less Doing team so successful as a team is that they can say no to me and they can tell me that I have a terrible idea and they can say we're not going to do that right now because it doesn't fit with our mission. Our vision can be driven forward, but it needs to be a shared vision and a vision compelling enough to warrant protection from every member of the team.

The final, salient part of the quote for me is the notion of non-attachment that we are capable of doing so much if we relinquish our control. We just need to access our insatiable curiosity and fearlessness. Participating in all that our entrepreneurial lives have to offer, means allowing things to be; that letting go isn't some pain-inducing exercise, but a shift in mindset from letting it go, to just letting it be. When we do this, we can all go from writing a sonnet to butchering a hog. Attachment doesn't mean that you are not engaged in the work. It's that we don't see ourselves at the center of that work. If you are presented with a problem, if a customer shits on your idea, you don't shut down. It's the idea, not you. If someone quits, you don't lash out, you thank them for their service and wish them well.

If you can remove ego and understand that you're creating an exciting thing for everyone to work on and if it doesn't work out, it doesn't mean you don't give a shit. It says you have an opportunity to create something new. So with the replaceable notion firmly rooted in your heart, the next idea will fuel your passion, impact your team and ultimately serve you, your family, your community, and the world.

You simply need to get out of your own way.

I hope I've given you a roadmap for that journey.

PODCAST WISDOM FROM REPLACEABLE

FOUNDERS

To date, I've done hundreds of podcasts, with the coolest people. I continue to be impressed by my guests ability to speak the truth and share their wisdom. I always ask the same question at the end of an episode, "What are your top 3 pieces of advice to become more effective?"

Text the word, PODCASTS to 33777 and I'll send you their collected wisdom, suitable for framing.

TECH STACK - MINDMAP

While I consider myself to be "tool agnostic", there are a few I simply could not live without.

Yes, I'm tool agnostic.

Yes, there's some stuff I couldn't live without.

Yes, the tech changes faster than my kids run.

So, send an email to oao@lessdoing.com with the subject TECHTOOLS and I happily send you my favorite tech tools organized in a spiffy mindmap.

Made in the USA
Monee, IL
06 February 2021

59641104R00066